Prepping for Beginners
Keys to Survive and Thrive

By Joe Paine

© **2014**

Are You Prepared? For almost anything? Or do you think that Prepping has to cost you a lot of money?

Well, I'm here to tell you that it doesn't! You can prepare you and your family for any situation without breaking the bank. Prepping doesn't have to be an expensive idea. There are tips and tricks you can take today to start prepping AND saving money.

If you are interested in learning how to protect your family from any and all of the inevitable disasters that could potentially happen, this book is your first step to learning how to prepare for any emergency situation.

Don't wait - Get started today!

Prepping for Beginners- Keys to Survive and Thrive

"If it weren't for the last minute, nothing would get done."
— Rita Mae Brown

"You cannot escape the responsibility of tomorrow by evading it
today."
— Abraham Lincoln

Prepping. Preparing your home, your family, and yourself to survive a catastrophic situation. What type of situation? Well, it could be anything. War. Terrorism. Natural disasters. Civil unrest. Power grids going down. An electro-magnetic pulse. There are more possible causes for a survival situation than most of us can even begin to imagine. So, what's the solution? Prepping!

To be completely honest, when I first heard about prepping, I thought it was all kinds of strange. I thought of crazy people with their tin-foil hats digging out underground bunkers and waiting for the end of the world while eating canned tuna for the rest of their lives. This was way back before Y2K hit.

I had to admit, though, on some level the whole thought of the "world coming to an end" scared me. The thought of an economic collapse or the threat of an EMP that shut everything that was electric down seemed overwhelming and very, very real. I thought I better get busy preparing, so I began to throw together some food, bottled water, blankets, and flashlight with lots of batteries, and called it good. Y2K came and went and nothing happened. Many people threw out their supplies and vowed never to "do that again".

As the years passed, I watched things unfolding in the news reports, and I began to see the urgency in preparing my family for whatever may come. I realized I needed to get myself and my family prepared for any number of situations that could cause an upheaval in society as we know it. There was one small problem. I wasn't rich – not by a long shot. I lived paycheck to paycheck. I had a family to feed and support. How on earth was I going to buy all the equipment that I started seeing on the lists I found from other peppers websites? I thought things were pretty hopeless.

Perhaps you are in the same position. Face it: it's hard to afford things in today's economy if you have a family of three or four (or more). With all the research I did, I found so much information on so many preppers websites that my head was swimming. How was I supposed to make sense of it all? I had to start sorting through the information and find what I could do for my family that I could afford. Through this process, I came across a lot of tips and tricks to help those of us who are on a budget.

Things don't have to look hopeless. You can still start prepping today, whether you're on minimum wage or you have plenty of money in the bank. Prepping principles work regardless of how much disposable income you have. The important thing is to resolve to start somewhere, and to start today. Hopefully, I can give you some basic strategies to start preparing your family without busting your budget. We will talk about the bare bones of prepping and how to decide what is affordable to you. Let's tackle this one subject at a time – so let's get started!

WATER

It seems like everyone starts with this subject. And why not? It's obviously the one thing that everybody needs to survive, regardless of anything else in their lives. Let me ask you this - have you ever tried to go three days without water? Two days? Even one full day without water? It's not pleasant. Going without water, even for a full day, is dangerous. You would risk terrible medical issues, if not death itself. Of all the things that should be on your list, the number one should be water.

It is essential for life – we all know that. But what do you do about water when you're prepping? Water is tough to store because of the volume and weight that it takes up. Plus, you also need to consider the shelf life of water as well. Will you buy bottled water? Big gallon jugs? Do you have property with a source of freshwater, like a river or stream? Do you live somewhere where you can collect rainwater safely and easily? Think about this for a moment - the average person needs at least a gallon of water a day to live (more if you include hygiene). If you have three or more people in your family, that's an awful lot of water. It adds up quickly!

You may be thinking - "where am I going to store all that?" It is a daunting task, but thankfully, it can be done. There are some simple and affordable answers to that. First, as most of us know, bottled water is readily affordable these days. You can pick up a case of 24 bottles for $5 or so at most grocery stores. If you buy one case every couple of weeks when you go grocery shopping, pretty soon you'll have plenty of bottles of water in your pantry. Of course, bottled water takes up a lot of space and weight, so depending on your pantry and living circumstances, it might not be the best option.

Another idea is to purchase larger water storage containers, where you can store 5, 10, or 20 gallons even. These can be a good option, but you will typically need to add chemicals to them to ensure the water doesn't go bad. Since the water is not stored in as secure an environment as sealed bottled water, you need to take steps to make sure that the water remains drinkable, even after longer periods of time. Adding chemicals to treat the water is one way of doing this. This can increase its shelf life for up to 5 years.

Another option is to invest in a water filter system for your home. You have to read specifics on each filter to find out what exactly they will filter and how many gallons they will produce. If it comes right down to it you can look in the camping section of your local department store. There you will find any number of affordable water filtration systems and also water treatment pills. These pills are extremely affordable and purify water simply by dropping a pill into your water source, but if you live in a city and you have no access to a water source that might be a problem.

If you have room on your property and you live in a climate that gets a lot of precipitation, setting up a rainwater collection system can be a great option as well. Usually this involves a series of pipes or drains that collect rainwater from your roof (or elsewhere) and funnel it into a giant container. You have to ensure that the container doesn't become contaminated and that nothing can get into it that isn't supposed to. But if you set it up properly, it can be a great source of fresh, clean water and, after the initial set-up, it is virtually free to keep collection water for as long as you want or need to.

Starting to think about water issues can be daunting. You have to consider how much you and your family will need, how much space you have to store the water, which method you will use (bottles, containers, freshwater, rainwater, filters, purification pills, etc.), and how to get everyone in the family involved with the plan. It can seem difficult to get started. But you have to start somewhere though! Procrastinating doesn't take care of you or your family in a dangerous situation, so resolve to start your prepping by focusing on water. Begin with bottled water. Buy a case and find somewhere to put it. Store it under your bed, in a closet, a basement, or a spare bedroom to start. Doing a little bit every chance you can is a whole lot better than doing nothing at all.

FOOD

After water, the other most important survival item is food. We can't last very long without water, it's true. It's also true that we can last a lot longer without food than water. But that doesn't mean that it's not important to think about food for survival. Far from it! After water, you really need to focus on your food prep – what you will store, where you will store it, and how much you will store. So, let's get to it.

There are many options for survival food on the market. What do you choose from without breaking the bank? MREs, Freeze-dried products, survival meal buckets with several meals in them, or do you store large amounts of basic ingredients to make things from scratch? Whatever you chose you must make sure it is something you will eat. Nothing depletes moral more than having to eat food that you have to force yourself to eat. There are some great products out there, but some of them extremely expensive. You need to find what will fit your family best. So how do you store up food without going into debt?

When I first started prepping, I began buying a little extra every time I went to the grocery store. I looked for things that were on sale and picked up things I knew my family would eat and things that would keep for a long time. Canned tuna and chicken, soups and chili, fruits and vegetables – we had enough canned food to feed an army. Many stores run the popular 10 for $10 sales on canned goods or boxed foods. I started purchasing 10 extra canned vegetables or canned fruit, Rice a Roni or other easy-fix boxed items – these are all great too. Be sure that you don't buy tomato-based products (they spoil easier) and you also have to be mindful about shelf life. A good way to get your children involved is to put them in charge of the food items in the pantry. Have them get a notebook and make sure all of the items are written down, along with their expiration date. Teach your kids to rotate food stocks (oldest items up front, newer in the back) and use up items that are close to their expiration date, and then replace them. This is a great way to get the whole family involved and your children will really learn about prepping through this experience.

Another great way to build up your pantry and save a lot of money at the same time is to buy rice, oats, sugar, and dry beans in bulk, if you have air tight containers to store them. Raman noodles are also cost effective and go a long way if you have kids. There are also many freeze-dried products out there that will provide the extra protein needed to sustain you. Also look for beef or turkey jerky and energy bars, as they are affordable if you buy in bulk and are time tested survival foods.

A word of caution when stocking your prepper's pantry: you really need to watch the sodium levels of the foods you are storing. Many of these canned or boxed or ready-to-eat products are absolutely packed with sodium. While essential for a preservative, it's not all that great for the blood pressure. Apart from canned meats and items like bars and jerky, try to stick with food items that can be made by just adding water. You don't want to buy things that require extensive cooking before they become edible. Based on the survival situation, you may have no power to cook, no way to start a fire to cook, or any other number of things. You want the easiest food options for those situations.

It bears repeating again, because I have made this mistake many times in my early prepping days - If you do plan on storing food for any extended period of time, make sure you rotate it over time! For instance dried milk can get weevils and water bottles can break down after a year and spring leaks (I learned those lessons the hard way). You also need to be absolutely sure that your containers are airtight and waterproof. Nothing is worse than thinking you are prepared when a disaster strikes and you find all the work had only resulted in something that you can't use.

Where you store your supplies is important as well. Having them off the cement floor lengthens shelf life, so try to get a pallet or even double pallet them. The best option for food or any supply storage is a closed cabinet with a domed roof. Why would that be important? If you live in an area where storms are prevalent, what would happen to your materials if it sustained flooding? They'd be completely ruined. Even in the Northern part of the United States, where I reside in a large city, anything could happen such as a water main break, unseasonable rains, or flooding due to melting snow. You really have to think about the area you live in and tailor your food storage for your specific situation. I mentioned that it would be a good idea to have something with a round or A-framed roof. If the roof is flat, it may allow for standing water and the opportunity for leaks. Protect your investments the best possible way that you can. You don't want to put time and effort and money into building a food pantry, only to have it ruined by water or bugs or anything else. Protect your investment and you'll save money in the long run!

SHELTER

When a disaster strikes or you find yourself and your family in a survival situation, where are you going to go? Are you going to try and flee for safety right away or are you going to hunker down in your current location and try to ride things out there?

This may be obvious question, but many people overlook it when they start thinking about prepping. You may be thinking that you could just stay in your house. While that may be true for most situations, sometimes bugging out is the only option you have left. Think about the wild fires out west. The fire spread quickly to subdivisions that left residents only hours at the most to grab things and evacuate. What would you do in that situation?

You need a bug out bag and you need a plan to stay in your home. This way, no matter what the situation is, you will be ready to stay or to go. Many books have been writing solely on bug out bags but the basic idea is that you need to pack a bag for each member of your family that will carry the essentials for your survival for 72 hours. This should be long enough for you to make it somewhere safe or for you to survive and then return to your home base. Typically a bug out bag will contain water, food, a first-aid kit, a weapon of some sort, and perhaps something that is specific to your region (such as cold weather clothes if you live in the north).

You can also pack supplies in your vehicle or nearby in case you have to camp out for a few days. Having a tent or two is not a bad idea. Also it would be good to have a few tarps, ropes, and other outdoor tools handy. Learning how to build a shelter in the great outdoors from scratch couldn't hurt. Learn how to build a fire. Learn how to treat wounds out in the open. What is that motto? Always be prepared. Taking a survival trip with your family is a great idea. A trial run to test the skills you learn is great to work out any problems ahead of time. This can be a great bonding experience for your family. It will also help to instill the survival values in your children that they will need. Nobody wants to think about what will happen when they aren't around any more, but as preppers, we need to face the cold hard truth that there will come a day when we won't be in the picture. Of course we will want our loved ones to carry on surviving without us, right? And how can we help ensure that they will be able to do that? Practice, practice, practice! Get out there as a family often and start sharing your survival skills. Make it a family tradition to go out once or twice every couple of months to practice. The more times you practice as a family, the easier survival will be when the real situation hits – with or without you.

GUNS, AMMO, AND WEAPONS

When a survival situation happens, we have no idea how the rest of the world will react. Will your neighbors be prepared? Will they become desperate to survive and maybe even have to resort to doing unimaginable things? Will you be ready for that situation if it ever happens, God forbid?

Self-defense is something that not everybody thinks about. You can have the best prepper's pantry in the world, with a great bug out bag, and an evacuation plan to beat all others. But none of that will matter one little bit if the first person with a weapon can come along and take it all away from you. There are many things to think about when we talk about self-defense. Should you have a gun? A knife? Know martial arts? How much, and how early, do you want to teach your children about protecting themselves? Do you need to spend a fortune on the latest and greatest gadgets to stay on top of trends and protect yourself? Or do old 'tried and true' methods of self-defense still work the best?

The most important thing I have ever read about guns is this: Having one gun that you know how to use well is worth more than having an entire safe full of guns that you can't hit a barn with. If you are experienced with guns, you know that there are many options to choose from. Educate yourself first before you make an investment. If you haven't been around guns, you not only need to do some research but you need to go to a local gun range and take a class.

Learn how to handle a weapon and learn which weapon is best for your personal situation. Actually shooting a gun will give you a feel for what is the right weapon for you. This should be applied for everyone in your household. Older children and teens can be taught respect and responsibility with guns, if taught properly and if taught often.

Other weapons on the market are crossbows, compound bows, knives, and many other options. I have a 3rd degree black belt in karate and encourage people to explore martial arts. I recommend a beginner's self-defense class for most of your family members, at the very least. Add this to the list a survival class. Knowing how to make a fire or make a shelter is just as important and having a gun. Your choices for self-defense will depend largely on your personal situation. If you live on an isolated lot in the country, your self-defense needs will be much different than if you live on the 20th floor of a high-rise condo in the middle of Chicago. Adapt your prepping experience and your self-defense regimen for your personal situation. Don't follow advice just because some guru says so. Think about what makes sense for you and your family, for your surroundings, and for your level of safety.

Always remember knowledge is the best weapon you can ever have. You can spend all the time in the world prepping, but if you don't know how to utilize your tools, you are still in danger.

MEDICAL SUPPLIES

What happens if you or one of your family members gets injured in a survival situation? What if you can't travel for help? What if hospitals are completely not functioning anyways? Will you know what to do? That's right – you need a first aid kit and you need to know how to use it!

A survival first aid kit is much more than just the first aid kit stuck in the drawer in your bathroom. This is about really thinking through emergencies and trying to cover your bases. Think about this scenario. The electricity has been out for weeks. You have a car but no gas. Your son was going down into the basement to get some supplies. You hear a crash and go running down the stairs only to find your son has fallen. His leg is broken. He has a gash across his arm. It is bleeding profusely and is deep. Do you know what to do? There is no one to call. No ambulance will come, and you don't have the gas to get to a hospital. Remember, knowledge is best weapon you have. Knowing first aid and lifesaving skills are extremely important. You can learn these in a class that can be taken at your local Red Cross or hospital. You can read first-aid manuals online or at the library and brush up on the basics. Knowing basic first aid and CPR can give your loved one a fighting chance if something happens in a survival situation.

As far as affordability – how can you get the best first-aid kit for the least amount of money? Well, to start, many dollar stores have bandages, band aides, first aid creams, peroxide and the like. Most department stores are carrying special first aid supplies in their camping sections. For instance there are packets that you can buy that will help stop a wound from bleeding. There are several different kinds. Many insect bite kits are available as well. You can also usually buy fairly extensive first-aid kits in most big stores. These will contain all of the necessary items in one convenient package.

Take caution though, when it comes to dollar store medications. You can buy certain supplies from dollar or discount stores, but don't try and save money on medications. Many are made in third world countries where there are no regulations. Just check your labels. Think through scenarios like the one I mentioned and see if you have the supplies needed. In the scenario that I described, you would need a way to provided compression to stop the bleeding, possibly a suture kit for stitches, a splint and crutches.

Among all of the dangers out there, almost nothing is more potentially deadly than an infection. From a bronchial infection or an infected cut, it could all add up to disaster if you have no means to fight it. How do you do that without a prescription and no pharmacy to fill it? If you could even get to a doctor, that is. There are many ways to fight infections that are not budget busting. I want you to use caution in this area. There are many side effects to any antibiotics and a potential for allergies. You know your family best, and you should know their medical history and allergies as well. Take all of this into account before you administer any type of antibiotics or any medicine at all, for that matter.

A great prepper's tip that I've learned, and something that not many people actually know or believe, has to do with medicine. Many of our human antibiotics are actually the same being given to fish and to birds. Seriously! Sure, the brand names and packaging are different, but when you get right down to it, the actual medicine inside is exactly the same as that which is given to humans. Now, no one should run out and by some Fish Flex or Bird Tetracycline instead of consulting your doctor and getting a proper prescription, of course. However, in an emergency, these will work exactly the same. Use the list below as a reference and decide which ones you can stock up on or which ones you'd like to research further (if you don't believe me!)

Fish Antibiotic = Human Antibiotic:
Fish-Mox = Amoxicillin 250mg
Fish-Mox Forte = Amoxicillin 500mg
Fish-Flex = Keflex 250mg
Fish-Flex Forte = Keflex 500mg
Fish-Zole = Metronidazole 250mg
Fish-Pen = Penicillin 250mg
Fish-Pen Forte = Penicillin 500mg

No, you might be thinking, "Man, I have been getting ripped off all these years by paying more money for my antibiotics!". Well, yes, we all have, to a certain degree, but you need to remember to just be careful. While, as preppers, we need to stockpile the things we need, you need to be absolutely sure that you don't sacrifice quality. Remember, we are stocking things for an emergency survival situation, NOT for every day, normal usage. While these fish antibiotics actually do the same things as the ones we pay a lot more money for, make sure you don't fall into the trap of purchasing medical supplies from other countries or for animals, just to save a quick buck. They do not have the same health standards in their plants as we do and some animal antibiotics just plain don't work on humans. Use the above list but don't stray from it. Don't buy an animal antibiotic that isn't on the above list just because you think it will work. They are NOT all the same. Just use caution. Knowledge is everything. You want to be prepared, but you don't want to put you or your family in danger, just to save a few dollars.

PERSONAL HYGIENE

This is an area of prepping that most people never even consider. But it's one thing that can really make morale sink quickly, if it's not addressed. Being stuck in close quarters without being able to take a shower or wash clothes can put you in some sticky situations. Failing to keep clean can also harbor bugs, viruses, and bacteria, and can make infections spread more quickly. Just because you're in a survival situation doesn't meant you don't need to take care of your sanitation needs – if anything, you need to focus on them more!

Having deodorant, powered, soap, toothpaste, toilet tissue and laundry detergent can mean all the difference in the world. Thankfully, these items all have really long shelf lives, so you can buy while they are on sale and store them away for whenever you will need them. While many of these are available at dollar stores, I urge you again to read the label. Tooth Paste made in Bangladesh for a dollar may not have a long shelf life as the one you might pay $.75 extra for the brand name the same with deodorant or powders.

We spend a great deal of time in our bathrooms. Whether bathrooms are still working after a survival event, or you find yourself forced to go outdoors in the open, a good supply of toilet paper is a must. If you are a woman, don't forget to think of feminine hygiene products. Again when you shop and you see that buy on get one free sale…use one and store the other. I tallied the bathroom products my family went through in one month and it was shocking, to say the least. We went through 24 rolls of toilet paper, 2 deodorants, 6 razors, 1 24 oz. bottle of shampoo, and 1 24 oz. conditioner, 1 pack of feminine napkins, 1 tube of tooth paste and a 100 pack of Q-Tips. You can see that if we had to live 6 months without the comforts of running water and electricity, the way we live would change, but the things we would need would not. Therefore, thinking about storing up on hygiene items is very important. Your morale will improve, your health will improve, and your family will find it much easier to survive and thrive together if you are all clean and healthy. So don't forget to think about this area as you plan your prepping!

OTHER SUPPLIES

So we've covered the basics that most people think of: water and food. We've talked about personal safety and first aid. We've also covered an item or two that most people don't think about when it comes to prepping. So, what else is left? Well, a lot!

It's pretty obvious that if the power is out due to a power outage, we will need a light source. Candles are the obvious quick fix. Those we can pick up at dollar stores to save our budget. Make sure you have matches or lighters on hand. Waterproof matches are a plus. A good trick to do is to have the birthday candles that you can't blow out. These are perfect for windy conditions. They stay lit until you soak them in water. The old-fashioned oil lamps that Grandpa had are a fantastic idea as well. Well, as long as you have a supply of lamp oil stored up. If not, make sure you stock up on lamp oil as well. The same applies to Coleman lanterns. Flashlights are another good option, especially if you have younger children (where open flames and hot oil could be very dangerous). If you choose to go with flashlights, make sure you have a large stock of batteries or use the rechargeable ones. You can recharge them by purchasing a solar cell panel and charger connected to a marine 12-volt battery. It will hold enough juice to charge cell phones, flashlights, rechargeable batteries, and radios.

There are some other common household items that you really need to think about as well. Garbage bags can be used for many things.

From a rain poncho to a liner in the toilet to be taken out and buried when filled, garbage bags are a must to have in your storage stockpile. They are usually cheap, as you can often find them on sale, so stock up whenever you see them advertised. Another group of items to think about are paper plates, disposable cutlery and cups. With water in high demand in a survival situation, wasting water for doing dishes is not a high priority. You'll want paper towels, as they can go a long way in cleaning up most any type of mess. Saran wrap is not only good for helping to store things, but it can be used in first aid to apply a pressure wrap or to seal a wound.

As far as cooking, I have found that propane works the best. It can be used with a smaller propane heater. I have three tanks that I rotate so that there are always two that are filled. Use caution when heating with propane indoors. Make sure the area is ventilated to ensure your family's safety and NEVER leave it unattended. Many homes have fireplaces so dropping money for a cord of wood to store in your back yard now and then is a cheap heat source. Not to mention cooking over a fire is as old as time itself. Whatever cooking method you choose, make sure all safety precautions are adhered too. You wouldn't want to add the burning of your home to the list of problems you are facing! As with other categories, the list of miscellaneous items will vary greatly depending on your personal situation. If you have babies or younger children, you'll obviously need different supplies (cloth diapers, bottles, a few toys, for example) than you would if you are on your own or you have teenagers. If you live somewhere that gets a lot of snow, you'll need to prep differently than if you live in the southwest and get a lot of sun and heat throughout the year. The prepping principles will remain the same, but the items you'll use to get there will be much different. So always take prepping advice and tailor it to your specific location and family situation.

BUGGING OUT

We mentioned the idea of creating a bug out bag earlier. It's not always possible to remain in your home during a survival situation, for any number of reasons. If you spend all of your time and energy on prepping to stay at home, and then the situation requires you to leave, you'll be out of luck. This is why it's so important to have a bug out plan as well.

If the police came to your door and told you that you had one hour to leave the area would you have a plan? Don't think it can happen to you? Think again. This past year we have seen evacuations from forest fires and from floods all across our countryside. Having a bug out plan means you can grab what you need to sustain your family for at least a week in less than twenty minutes.

There are prepared bug out bags that you can purchase, but it's just as fun to make your own, if you have the time. I used to back pack in Northern Michigan. I have a really nice lightweight backpack and some camping gear already. I decided to turn it into a game with my kids. We sat down and made a list of what we thought we would need. I put my fourteen-year-old son in charge of the list. He was to make sure everything got put into it, and cross things off as we gathered or purchased them. They thought of many things that we as a family had not talked about yet. I had racked my brain of all the necessities that I forgot something that was very important. They came up with three things to entertain us. Bugging out can stress kids out. Something as simple as a deck of cards, an extra pad of paper and a pencil, and a rubber racket ball/tennis ball will take up very little space and yet can provide hours of fun.

Bugging out is something you need to plan for and a really easy way to get the entire family involved in the prepping process. You can even do practice bug out days, where you pretend you have 20 minutes to get everything together, get everyone and their things into a car, and leave your house. You can stretch it into a more realistic weekend and then go camping for a couple of a days with your bug out gear, to show your family what it would really be like if you were forced to bug out. Not only is this really useful as a practice scenario, it can also be a lot of fun and really foster family togetherness. So start working on your bug out bags now, get your evacuation plan in order, and start practicing to bug out – you never know when you might need to!

IMPORTANT TIPS TO REMEMBER

The following are some more things to consider as you are prepping:

1. Do not post pictures of money or gold or your preps on Social Media. If you do, you might get some unwelcome visitors to your home or very nosey neighbors.

2. Make sure that your preparations are not against the law. If you have any doubt about this, make sure that you don't go bragging about that "new" unregistered semi-automatic hidden in the house.

3. In the event of a major disaster, there will likely be hordes of "non-preppers" running around looking to take away the things that you have been storing up. This is something that you will need to be prepared for.

Remember these rules!

1. **Trust no one that you do not personally know**. Even the little old man or granny down the road will rat on you if they get hungry enough in a crisis.

2. **Keep your prepping to yourself**. Again, do not tell anyone that doesn't need to know that you are prepping. If they know you have stores of food, where do you think they will think of first when all

hell breaks loose? The Department of Homeland Security thinks of people with stockpiles of food and weapons as potential domestic terrorists. So if you don't want them knocking on your door, then you need to keep quiet.

3. **Don't share any prepping articles on any form of social media**. Don't draw attention to yourself by posting prepping articles or discussing the topic on the website. You may think you are educating your friends, but in reality, you are just letting them know of your actions and plans. Not to mention what you put on the Internet stays on the Internet and can be traced back to your computer's IP address. Better safe than sorry.

4. **Make sure boxes are not labeled with the company name if your order emergency supplies**. Most companies will publish this in their ordering information. You don't want to tip off the UPS driver that you just received a year's worth of freeze-dried food. If it's really obvious what's inside, it might not actually make it to your doorstep. I'll say it again: Better safe than sorry.

5. **Do not tell anyone (besides family and support group) what you are up to**. You don't tell anyone that is not in your immediate family group. Today, families can get downright nasty with each other. Add the fact that your sisters in laws nephew is need of food! Well, emotions will boil over. You will have to have to courage to say "no" to people in need just to feed your kids. As selfish as that

may seem, it will be a necessity. Did they not have the same opportunity to prep as you did? I know it sounds harsh.

As the son of a minister, I often think back to the biblical story of Noah and the ark. He warned the people for 100 years that it was going to rain and to prepare. The laughed at him and called him crazy, fruit cake, doomsday preacher, and rolled their eyes at him. Kind of sound familiar? Well, when the rain started, Noah and his family, with all that they had prepped for, including all those animals, were safe in the ark and the door was shut to those who wouldn't listen. I often wonder what Noah and his family went through when his neighbors were pounding on the sides of the ark as the floodwaters rose and people began to drown. We fluff the story up for Sunday school lesson, but in all actuality Noah had the same responsibility we have. He heard the warnings. He prepped for the coming storm. He warned all those that he could. He kept his family safe. BUT he still had to have the courage to stand strong when all around him chaos was prevailing.

Saying "No" may be the hardest thing you might ever have to do and prepping yourself mentally for that is just as important as anything else.

6. **Be alert to what others are saying**. I was riding the city bus the other day and a group of passengers were talking about prepping. They had seen some prepping show on television and, of course,

now thought that it was the greatest idea ever. One was bragging about how he had this and that stored and was ready for anything. The other two began talking about their weapons. Another lady was saying they were all crazy. They kept getting louder and louder. The gentleman I was sitting next to laughed and stated that when the trouble hit the fan, he knew exactly whose house he was headed to. You don't want to be that house. Don't get drawn into discussions about prepping that will goad you into spilling the beans about your prepping work. It's simply not worth it.

OTHER THINGS TO CONSIDER

1. Get Out Of Debt – Prepping shouldn't cost you an arm and a leg. And you absolutely should not go into debt, just to prep. Someone I know did the exact opposite of this. They got as many credit cards as they could qualify for and went and maxed them out, buying all of the latest, expensive prepping gear they could find. They reasoned that if an economic collapse was coming then things like debts and credit wouldn't matter. As tempting as that may sound - Don't do it. Eliminate your debt and get away from using plastic all together. Credit is traceable. The less attention you bring to yourself, the better off you and your family will be.

2. Find New Sources of Income - This is simple. The more income you have, the more money you can use on preparing. The more you are able to use on prepping, the better off you'll be. If you have the time, energy, or means to find a part-time job, do it. Your family and prepping pantry will thank you later.

3. Reduce Your Expenses - If you are living paycheck to paycheck, then trying to prep might bust your budget. Look at ways to cut unnecessary expenses. Do you really need a new smartphone with a $150/month plan? Or would that money be better spent on building up a pantry? Do you need the full cable package, with HBO and 100 different sports channels? Or would it be smarter to use that money to build bug out bags for you and your family? When you boil it down, the choices seem obvious. Reduce your unnecessary expenses and your prepping will benefit from it.

4. Learn to Grow Your Own Food – "Easier said than done", you're thinking. But really, it's not that difficult. This is possible even if you live in an apartment. Get creative in your thinking and do some research to see what you can grow in large flower boxes on your balcony. If you are fortunate enough to have a yard or some land, you should definitely think about growing some of your own produce. Next, learn how to preserve what you grow. Canning and vacuum sealing food are awesome skills to learn and to teach to your kids. Not only that but it's much more cost-effective to build up your prepper's pantry with homegrown and home-processed food than it is to just buy every food item. It'll save you money in the long-run and it's a heck of a lot better for your health than some things that prepper's buy.

5. Make Sure You Have A Reliable Water Supply - I mentioned this before, but it's worth mentioning again and again. I live in a large city that is one of the five most dangerous places to live in America. As I have been writing this book, I seriously have heard gunshots from the neighborhood not far from my house. Can you imagine the chaos that would happen if the city water was shut off for even a few days? What about a few weeks? Can you imagine the chaos that most cities around the world would descend into in that situation? Having a water supply could mean the difference between life and death for you and your family. Many, many people will not be prepared for such an event. Make sure that you are one of the few who is ready to survive and thrive.

6. Buy Land - This might seem expensive at first, but having that cabin somewhere apart from where you live might be the safest place to be. If your current area is unlivable, you need somewhere to escape to. Sure, some of us can survive out in the open. But for how long? And what if you have a bigger family? If you can get a place outside of the city or in a different area of the state, you'll truly be prepared to handle any situation.

7. Get Off The Grid - You might be thinking, "Oh, this has gone too far. This is all way beyond my little family." Think again. Do your own research. Have you ever Googled yourself? You might be amazed at what people can find out about you in just a few minutes. Do you really want or need all of that information out there in the public sphere? It certainly won't help you in a survival situation and it may even be detrimental. So try to keep things to a minimum in that regard, and you'll thank yourself later.

8. Get Educated and Stay Flexible – Knowledge is power. Learn what you can as you go. The world of prepping information out there is huge! If you try to take it all in at once, you will get overwhelmed and quit. Just try to learn a little bit at a time, using the best way you can to prevent yourself for being caught off guard.

Ask yourself the following questions and, in your search for the answers, you will learn more about yourself and your situation and what things you really need to focus on.

1. **What am I preparing for?**
2. **Am I going to bug in or bug out?**
3. **Can I defend my family, property and preps?**
4. **Do I have enough to feed my family until order is restored?**
5. **How will I heat my home?**
6. **How will I keep clean?**
7. **How will I provide light and electricity?**
8. **How will I keep up on information and communicate with the outside world?**
9. **What do I have to offer others?**
10. **How will I fight off boredom?**

I hope I have offered enough tips to get you and your family started on your prepping journeys. There really isn't any reason that you can't begin to prepare for a survival situation, even if you have to pinch your pennies. If your head is swimming like mine was when I first began to inquire about prepping, relax. It's okay. I think we all were at that point at first. The list of supplies and the things that need to be done can seem endless. But it doesn't have to be that way.

My best advice is to take it all in chunks. Do your prepping in bits and pieces. Buy a little here and there as you can afford. Cut out those extra expenses, or delay the vacation to look into purchasing the bigger items that you need. Prepping takes time, energy, and planning. Draw up a game plan that covers what you will do in the months and in the years ahead. In the end you have to remember you are protecting you and your family. What you do from this point on is totally up to you.

A survival situation can strike at any time. It may be from the weather, flood or fire, economic collapse, or any number of scenarios. Your goal is to be prepared to survive and thrive in any of these events. Take the steps needed. Follow some of these tips. Educate yourself. Talk to other preppers about their experiences. They might be able to share what worked for them and some pitfalls to avoid. If you have kids, turn it into a fun time to grow together and stay together.

Most importantly, and above all else, do not procrastinate. Start today! Even if you just do one little, tiny thing, do it today. I can guarantee you that if you start today, with something, anything, you will be prepared. That is what this is all about! Good luck, fellow preppers!

www.ingramcontent.com/pod-product-compliance
Lightning Source LLC
Chambersburg PA
CBHW061931280526
45787CB00004B/1568